MAKING
PICTURE
FRAMES

Written by Linda Hendry and Lisa Rebnord
Illustrated by Linda Hendry

KIDS CAN PRESS

For Liz — LH
With love for my mom and dad, Jean and Arthur Rebnord — LR

Text copyright © 1998 by Linda Hendry and Lisa Rebnord
Illustrations copyright © 1998 by Linda Hendry
First U.S. edition 1999

KIDS CAN DO IT and the 📖 logo are trademarks of Kids Can Press Ltd.

Published in Canada by   Published in the U.S. by
Kids Can Press Ltd.   Kids Can Press Ltd.
29 Birch Avenue   85 River Rock Drive, Suite 202
Toronto, ON M4V 1E2   Buffalo, NY 14207

Edited by Elizabeth MacLeod
Designed by Karen Powers
Photography by Frank Baldassarra
Printed in Hong Kong by Wing King Tong Co. Ltd.

CM 98 0 9 8 7 6 5 4 3 2 1

Canadian Cataloguing in Publication Data

Hendry, Linda
Making picture frames

(Kids Can do it)
ISBN 1-55074-505-0

1. Picture frames and framing — Juvenile literature.
I. Rebnord, Lisa. II. Title. III. Series.

N8550.H38 1998   j749'.7   C98-930341-1

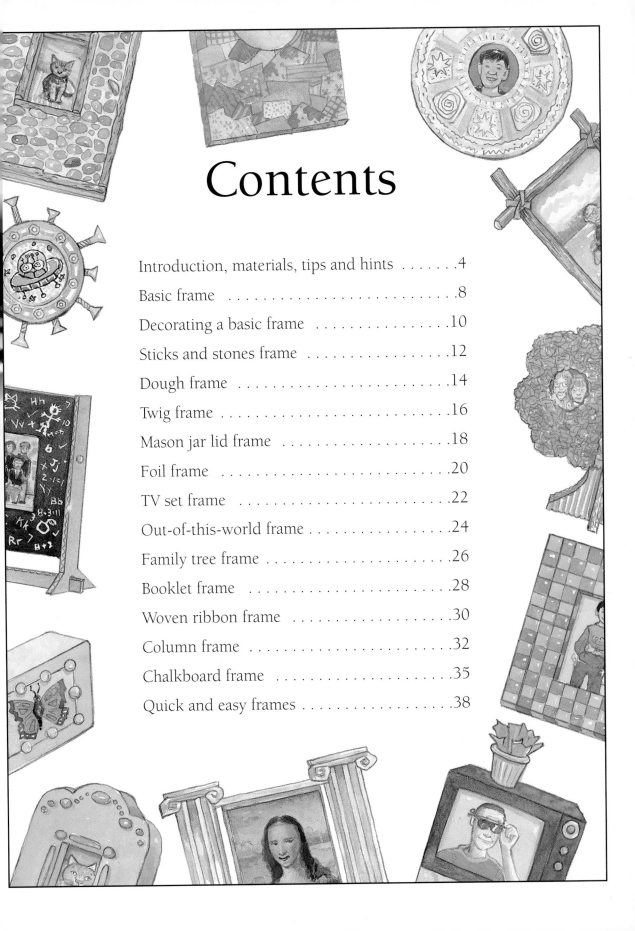

Contents

Introduction

A frame is the finishing touch that makes a good painting look great. But you can frame more than just paintings or drawings. Try putting a frame around photos, postcards, baseball cards, stamps, pressed flowers, mirrors — there's no end to the things you can frame. This book will show you how to turn easily found items into fabulous frames. You'll make frames to decorate your room, to display a special picture, or to give as a one-of-a-kind gift. Have fun!

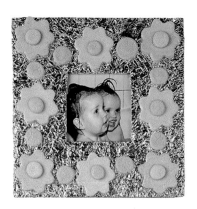

MATERIALS

Most of the materials you'll need for making the frames in this book can be found around your home.

CARDBOARD

You will need both corrugated and light cardboard for many of the projects in this book.

Large boxes used to ship heavy items are usually made from corrugated cardboard. Most grocery stores can give you a box to use. A medium-sized corrugated cardboard box will supply more than enough cardboard for any frame in this book.

Cereal or tissue boxes are made from light cardboard. A cereal box will provide you with enough cardboard to make most frames.

Plan your frames so that the unprinted side of the cardboard is the side you decorate.

GLUE

White glue attaches items permanently and dries clear.

SCISSORS AND UTILITY KNIVES

You can do most of the cutting in this book using a pair of sharp scissors, but you will get a straighter edge if you use a utility knife and a metal-edged ruler. Be sure to have an adult help you if you use a utility knife. Always protect the surface you are cutting on with a piece of corrugated cardboard. Make several light cuts with the knife rather than pressing hard.

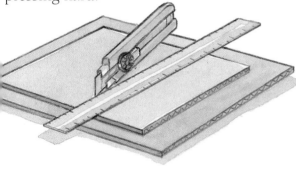

It is easier to fold cardboard and paper if you score the fold lines first. To score, lay a metal ruler along the line to be folded and make a very light cut along the edge of the ruler with a utility knife. Do not cut completely through the cardboard or paper.

PAINTS AND BRUSHES

Acrylic craft paints are inexpensive, come in many bright colors, and give a smooth finish to your frame. They dry quickly so place just as much as you will need onto a piece of waxed paper.

Small brushes work best for painting detail. Bigger brushes are good for painting larger areas or applying papier-mâché. Don't let paint dry on your brushes. Clean them with water between colors. When you are finished your project, clean your brushes with soap and then rinse them well.

TIPS

CUTTING THE PHOTO OPENING

The photo opening of your frame can be any shape. Try making it a square, a circle, a star or a heart shape. To design the opening, place a piece of tracing paper or tissue paper over the photo you are framing. On the paper, draw a shape that is slightly smaller than your photo. Place the paper on your frame front and use a pin to poke holes around the pattern. Remove the paper and cut out the opening using the pinpricks as a guide.

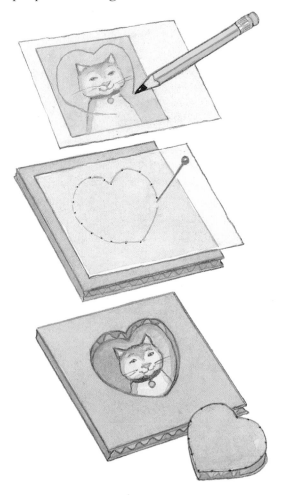

ATTACHING PHOTOS

Some of the frames in this book will hold your photos securely when you slide them into place. For others, you will need to attach the photos using one of the following methods.

Glue

Squeeze a thin line of white glue along the edges of the back of your photo. Don't use too much glue — it could make your photo buckle. Your photo will be attached permanently, so be sure you won't want to remove it later. You can also use a glue stick to attach your photo.

Tape

Place pieces of double-sided tape or loops of sticky tape in each corner of the back of your photo. Place your photo in position and press firmly to attach it.

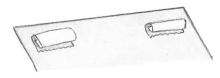

Photo corners

You can buy self-adhesive photo corners at most photo shops.

DISPLAYING FRAMES

• To make your frame stand on its own, make an easel back. Cut out a cardboard triangle that's as tall as your frame and that has a base a little narrower than your frame. Cut off the top third of the triangle and score a line as shown. Apply glue above the score line and center the stand on the frame back, lining it up with the bottom edge of the frame. Let the glue dry. Cut a thin strip of paper, fold it as shown and glue it in place.

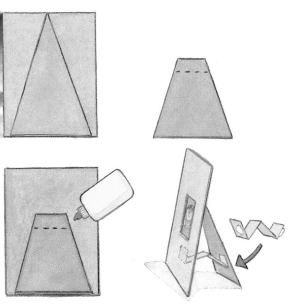

• To hang your frame, cut a length of cord and tie a knot at each end. Form the cord into a loop and attach it to the frame back by gluing a strip of construction paper just above the knots, as shown.

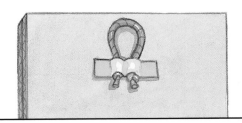

HINTS

• Gather all your materials together before you start.

• Check with your parents before you cut or glue any photos.

• Protect your work surface with newspaper.

• Measurements are given in both metric and imperial, which differ slightly. Choose one measurement system and use it for the entire project.

• The instructions for some of the frames in this book call for a specific size of photo. When a small photo is required, use a wallet-sized photo — the kind you get in a school photo package. A medium-sized photo would be a 9 cm x 13 cm (3 ½ in. x 5 in.) or a 10 cm x 15 cm (4 in. x 6 in.) snapshot.

• And remember, you can use postcards, stamps, drawings or whatever you like in place of a photo.

Basic frame

With these instructions, you can make a frame for any size of photo.

YOU WILL NEED

- a photo of any size

- corrugated cardboard, 2 pieces at least 10 cm (4 in.) longer and wider than your photo

- light cardboard about the same size as the corrugated cardboard

- masking tape, a ruler, a pencil, scissors or utility knife, white glue

1 To make the frame front, tape the photo in the center of one piece of corrugated cardboard. Decide how wide you want the border on all sides of the photo to be, and mark the width at two points on each side. Draw the border and cut out the frame front.

2 At each corner of your photo make two marks as shown, each 0.5 cm (¼ in.) in from the corner.

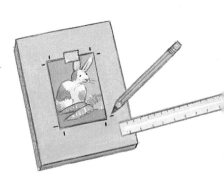

3 Remove your photo from the frame front and use your ruler to draw lines connecting the marks. Cut along these lines to cut out the photo opening.

4 To make the frame back, place the frame front on the other piece of corrugated cardboard, trace around the outside edge and cut out the shape.

6 Glue a spacer along the outside edge of each long side of the frame back. Trim the third spacer to fit between the first two spacers and glue it in place along the outside edge.

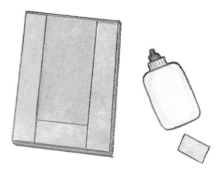

5 From the piece of light cardboard, measure and cut out three strips as long as the longest sides of your frame front and 0.5 cm (¼ in.) narrower than the border around the photo opening. These are called spacers (when your frame is finished, they provide space between the frame front and back for your photo).

7 Apply glue to the spacers and place the frame front on the frame back, lining up the edges. Place heavy books on top of the frame and leave it to dry for an hour. If you plan to decorate your frame by wrapping it in paper or covering it in collage or papier-mâché, see page 10 before you glue the frame's front to its back.

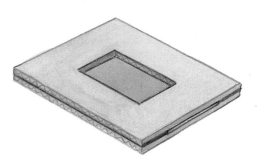

Turn the page for some great decorating ideas for your frame.

Decorating
a basic frame

*Now that you've made a basic frame,
it's time to decorate it.*

*You can wrap your frames in gift wrap,
comics, or even fabric.*

1 Cut a piece of paper that is 2.5 cm (1 in.) larger than your frame on each side.

2 Center the frame front on the paper. Fold the paper over one side of the frame and fasten it with tape. Fold the paper over the opposite side of the frame and pull gently to smooth the paper. Fasten it with tape. Fold in each corner diagonally. Fold over the two remaining sides and tape them down.

3 Use a ruler to draw a diagonal line connecting one corner of the frame opening to the opposite corner. Repeat with the remaining corners and cut along the lines.

4 Fold back the flaps of paper. Trim them if necessary, and tape them in place. You can also wrap the frame back before gluing it to the frame front.

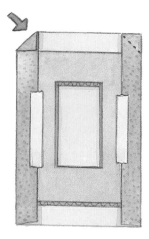

PAPIER-MÂCHÉ

Covering your frame with papier-mâché will hide its unfinished edges.

1 Mix 12 spoonfuls of flour, 12 spoonfuls of water and 3 spoonfuls of salt and stir into a smooth paste. (This mixture will keep in the refrigerator for several days if it is covered.)

2 Dip small strips of newspaper into the paste and apply them to your frame front in layers. Be sure to wrap the strips neatly around all edges. Or instead of dipping the strips, use a paintbrush to apply the paste to your frame, then add a layer of paper strips and brush more paste on top. Cover the frame with two or three layers. Add a final layer of tissue paper strips using the paintbrush method to give your frame a smooth surface for painting.

Try gluing small balls of crumpled paper or shapes cut from corrugated cardboard to your frame front before you cover it with several layers of tissue paper and paste. Be sure the frame front is completely dry before gluing it to the frame back.

COLLAGE

You might like to cover your frame with pictures cut from magazines or with small strips of colorful gift wrap.

1 Mix 6 spoonfuls of white glue and 3 spoonfuls of water. Use a paintbrush to spread the glue mixture on a small area of your frame, then apply your pictures or paper strips. Continue until your frame front is covered. Wrap the pictures or paper strips neatly around all edges and let your frame front dry.

2 Brush on a final layer of glue mixture to seal your collage. Be sure the frame front is completely dry before gluing it to the frame back.

PAINT

Try using a piece of sponge or a crumpled plastic bag to apply paint to your finished frame. Cut designs into potatoes, erasers or corks, dip them into paint, and stamp the designs onto your frame.

DECORATIONS

Ask your parents for old jewelry, beads, buttons, small toys, yarn or lace, pasta, or dried beans, and use white glue to attach them to your frame.

Sticks and stones frame

Nature photos look great in this frame.

YOU WILL NEED

- a photo of any size
- a basic frame (see page 8)
- straight twigs, about 12
- small pebbles, about 375 mL (1 ½ c.)
- 50 mL (¼ c.) all-purpose flour
- 50 mL (¼ c.) salt
- 5 mL (1 tsp.) black pepper
- a piece of corrugated cardboard, about 23 cm x 30 cm (9 in. x 12 in.)
- white glue, 2 empty margarine tubs, a spoon, a paintbrush, a dishcloth

1 Break the twigs into pieces long enough to fit along the outside edges of your frame front. You may want two or three pieces on each side. Glue the twigs in place. Arrange more twigs around the photo opening. Glue them in place.

2 Fill the area inside the twig borders with pebbles. Glue them in place and let the glue dry.

3 Combine the flour, salt and pepper in a margarine tub. Gradually add 125 mL (½ c.) of water, stirring until smooth. Add 15 mL (1 tbsp.) of white glue and mix well.

4 Use the paintbrush to dribble the glue mixture into the spaces between the pebbles. Continue until the glue is about 0.25 cm (⅛ in.) thick and no cardboard is showing. Let it dry overnight.

5 When the frame is dry, wet the dishcloth and gently clean any dried glue off the pebbles.

6 Mix 15 mL (1 tbsp.) each of white glue and water in a margarine tub. Paint this mixture over the dried glue to seal it. Let it dry for about one hour.

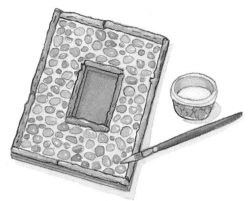

7 Attach an easel back to your frame using the corrugated cardboard and following the directions on page 7.

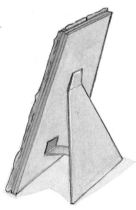

8 Insert your photo in the frame.

Dough frame

This frame is colorful and easy to make.

- 500 mL (2 c.) all-purpose flour
- 250 mL (1 c.) salt
- 200 mL (¾ c. + 2 tbsp.) water
- 30 mL (2 tbsp.) vegetable oil
- 2 packages of unsweetened drink mix, each 6 g (1 tbsp.) and different colors
- a small photo • acrylic varnish
- a piece of corrugated cardboard, about 13 cm x 18 cm (5 in. x 7 in.)
- a piece of light cardboard, about 13 cm x 18 cm (5 in. x 7 in.)
- a large mixing bowl, a mixing spoon, 2 plastic bags, waxed paper, a rolling pin, a table knife, a baking sheet, a pencil, scissors or utility knife

1 Combine the flour and salt in the bowl. Gradually stir in the water and vegetable oil and mix well.

2 Place half of the dough on a lightly floured surface. Knead in one package of drink mix. Repeat with the remaining dough and drink mix. Wrap each piece of dough in a plastic bag and refrigerate for 30 minutes.

3 Place a piece of waxed paper on your work surface and roll out one piece of dough until it is 0.5 cm (¼ in.) thick.

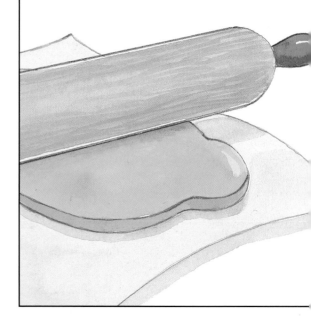

4 Decide what shape you want your frame to be and cut it out with the table knife. The frame should be at least 5 cm (2 in.) taller and wider than your photo. Put the extra dough back in the plastic bag so it won't dry out. Cut out an opening for your photo (see page 6).

5 Use the second color of dough to decorate your frame. Roll balls or ropes with your fingers, or use small cookie cutters to make shapes. Lightly press the decorations onto your frame.

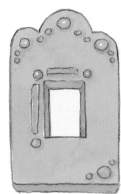

6 Heat your oven to 120°C (250°F). Carefully transfer your frame on the waxed paper to the baking sheet. Ask an adult to help you place the sheet on the middle rack in your oven and bake your frame for about four hours. If you prefer, let the frame dry at room temperature — this will take several days.

7 When the frame is completely cool and dry, brush on at least two coats of acrylic varnish. Let it dry.

8 To make the frame back, place your frame on the piece of corrugated cardboard, trace around it and cut out the shape. Following steps 5 and 6 on page 9, cut out three strips of light cardboard for spacers and attach the spacers and frame back to the dough frame. Attach an easel back following the directions on page 7.

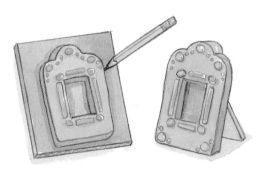

9 Insert your photo in the frame.

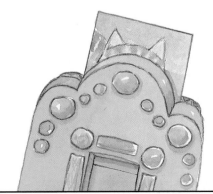

Twig frame

Camping photos or postcards from a trip to the mountains look especially good in a rustic twig frame.

YOU WILL NEED

- a small- or medium-sized photo
- a piece of corrugated cardboard that's the same size as your photo
- 4 twigs, each one 5 cm (2 in.) longer than the sides of your photo
- a piece of ribbon or twine 81 cm (32 in.) long
- scissors or utility knife, white glue

1 Trim each corner of the cardboard as shown.

2 Glue a long twig to each long side of the cardboard as shown.

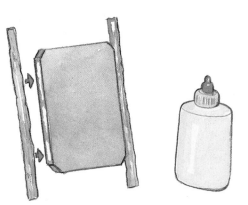

3 Place a short twig along each short edge of the cardboard and glue them to the other twigs where they touch. Let the glue dry.

4 Cut the ribbon or twine into four
20 cm (8 in.) long pieces.

5 Thread a piece of ribbon behind
the twigs at the top left corner as
shown. Cross the ribbon over the front
of the twigs and then wrap it to the
back. Tie a tight knot. Trim the ends of
the ribbon and place a dab of glue on
the knot to secure it. Repeat on the
remaining corners.

6 Attach the photo to the frame (see
page 6). Trim the corners of the
photo if necessary. Make a hanger or an
easel for your frame (see page 7).

OTHER IDEAS

Try making this frame using pencils,
cinnamon sticks or even dried grasses
tied into bundles.

Mason jar lid frame

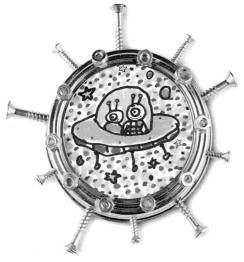

Mason jar lids are inexpensive and easy to find at hardware stores.

YOU WILL NEED

- a standard mason jar lid
- a piece of corrugated cardboard that's just larger than the lid
- a short piece of 2 in. x 4 in. wood
- a hammer and a nail
- a picture that's just larger than the lid
- 5 screws, each 3 cm (1¼ in.) long
- 5 screws, each 2 cm (¾ in.) long
- 10 small bolts or other interesting bits of hardware
- a cloth tape measure, a pencil, scissors, white glue

1 Place the lid on the cardboard and trace around its rim. Cut out the circle. This will be your frame back.

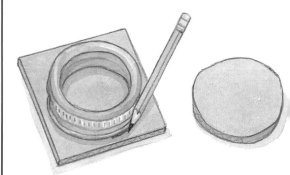

2 On the rim of the lid, mark ten evenly spaced points 2.3 cm (⅞ in.) apart.

3 Ask an adult to place the lid on the piece of wood as shown and use the hammer and nail to punch a hole through each point.

4 Trim your picture to fit the frame back and insert the frame back and the picture into the lid.

5 Insert a long screw into the hole at the top of the lid and turn it three or four times. Do the same with a short screw in the next hole. Alternate long and short screws all the way around the lid.

6 On the front of the frame, carefully dab glue between each screw. Place a bolt on each dab of glue. Make a hanger or an easel for your frame (see page 7).

OTHER IDEAS

• To make a lacy frame, weave ribbon through a 1 m (3 ft.) piece of lace. Pull on the ribbon to gather in the lace, place the lace around a lid and tie the ribbon in a bow. Insert your picture and frame back into the lid.

• To make a fuzzy frame, wrap pipe cleaners around a lid, then insert your frame back and picture.

Foil frame

Don't throw away those foil containers! Recycle them into great picture frames.

YOU WILL NEED

- a foil container, such as a pie plate
- 2 pieces of corrugated cardboard larger than the bottom of the container
- a ballpoint pen
- a small- to medium-sized photo
- a sheet of construction paper
- scissors, masking tape, white glue

1 Place the pie plate on the cardboard and trace around the bottom. Cut out the shape and set it aside. This will be your frame back.

2 Ask an adult to cut off the rim of the pie plate. The edge may be sharp, so be careful!

3 Make a cut from the edge of the pie plate to its bottom. Continue to make cuts about 2.5 cm (1 in.) apart, around the edge of the plate.

4 Fold out the flaps you just cut so that the pie plate lies flat.

5 To design the opening for your photo, see page 6. There may be a pattern pressed into the bottom of the pie plate that can help you decide on the shape of your opening. Use the pen to draw the shape onto the bottom of the plate. Cut it out.

6 Using the pen, practice drawing patterns on the foil shape you just cut out. Place the foil on the second piece of cardboard and draw dots and squiggly or broken lines. Don't poke through the foil.

7 When you're ready to decorate your frame, place the pie plate on the cardboard and use the pen to draw your pattern on the bottom of the plate.

8 Turn the pie plate over. This is the front of your frame. Tape your photo to the back of the frame so it shows through the opening, then lay your frame face down again.

9 Set the cardboard backing in place, fold the flaps over it and tape them down. Cut out a piece of construction paper that's a little smaller than the frame and glue it to the back. Make a hanger or an easel for your frame (see page 7).

TV set frame

Here's your chance to decide what should be on TV!

YOU WILL NEED

- a small cardboard box, about 15 cm x 15 cm x 7.5 cm (6 in. x 6 in. x 3 in.)
- papier-mâché (see page 11)
- 4 pushpins
- a medium-sized photo
- a piece of black construction paper
- a piece of clear acetate that's the same size as your photo
- a foil pie plate • thumbtacks
- aluminum foil
- a small plastic cream container
- 3 squares of green tissue paper, each 10 cm x 10 cm (4 in. x 4 in.)
- sticky tape, white glue, paint, a paintbrush, scissors, a pencil

1 Tape the box shut. Cover it completely with a thin layer of papier-mâché. Let it dry.

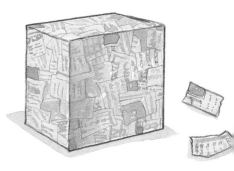

2 To make the feet for your TV, put a drop of white glue in each corner of the bottom of the box. Poke a pushpin through each drop of glue into the box. Let the glue dry. Paint the box.

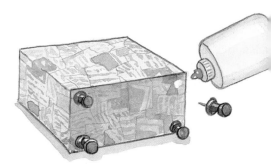

3 To make the TV screen, cut out a piece of construction paper 2.5 cm (1 in.) shorter and narrower than the box. Cut out a piece of acetate slightly smaller than the construction paper.

4 Cut a screen-shaped opening in the center of the construction paper. Center the acetate on the paper frame and fasten it with tape.

5 Squeeze a line of glue along the bottom and sides of the taped side of the paper frame. Place it on the front of the box at the top left corner. Leave the top edge unglued so you can slide in your photo.

6 To make the TV knobs, cut out a circle from the pie plate that's 2 cm (¾ in.) in diameter. Glue it to the front of the TV, beside the screen. Push a thumbtack through the center of the foil circle into the box. Make more knobs using different sizes of foil circles, or use just the thumbtacks.

7 To make the speaker, cut a strip of aluminum foil that fits across the bottom of the TV, as shown. Attach it to the box with glue. Insert your photo.

8 To make a potted plant, paint the outside of the cream container. Squeeze some glue into it. Poke the eraser end of your pencil into the center of one of the tissue paper squares, scrunch the tissue around the pencil and push it into the glue. Repeat with the other squares of tissue paper.

OTHER IDEAS

• Use bottle lids and caps to look like snack dishes.

• Paint a small eraser to look like a remote control.

• Paint a small piece of cardboard to look like a TV program guide.

Out-of-this-world frame

Make a frame with an outer space theme, or use your imagination to create a world of your own.

YOU WILL NEED

• corrugated cardboard,
a piece 30 cm x 40 cm (12 in. x 16 in.) and
a piece 13 cm x 18 cm (5 in. x 7 in.)

• scraps of construction paper

• a photo that's 13 cm x 18 cm
(5 in. x 7 in.) or smaller

• a ruler, a pencil, scissors or utility knife,
glue, 2 clothespins, paint, paintbrushes

1 Place the large piece of cardboard printed side up (if applicable) with its short sides at the top and bottom. Draw two lines across the cardboard, one 5 cm (2 in.) from the bottom and one 8 cm (3 in.) from the bottom.

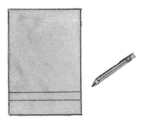

2 Mark a point 8 cm (3 in.) from each end of the lines you just drew. Draw two lines 13 cm (5 in.) long through the points toward the top of the cardboard.

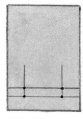

3 Add these lines and shapes:

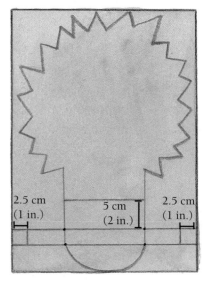

2.5 cm
(1 in.)

5 cm
(2 in.)

2.5 cm
(1 in.)

4 Cut out the frame. Score the lines where shown. Be careful not to cut through the cardboard.

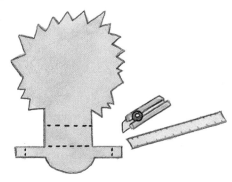

5 Turn the frame over and fold as shown.

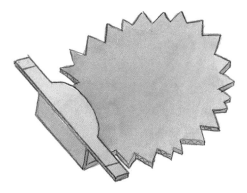

6 Fold the tabs back and glue them to the inside of the frame. Hold them in place with the clothespins until they dry.

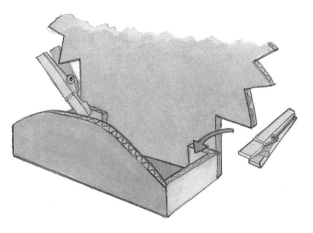

7 Cut out stars, rockets, planets and aliens from scraps of cardboard or construction paper. Paint the frame and the decorations. To make the decorations really stand out, glue several small squares of cardboard to the back of each one before gluing them to the frame.

8 Paint the small cardboard rectangle, attach your photo to it (see page 6), then place it in the frame.

Family tree frame

You can display as many as eight photos on this leafy frame.

YOU WILL NEED

- 8 small photos
- a piece of white paper, 25 cm x 35 cm (10 in. x 14 in.)
- 4 pieces of corrugated cardboard, each 25 cm x 35 cm (10 in. x 14 in.)
- 4 sheets of green tissue paper, cut into 5 cm x 5 cm (2 in. x 2 in.) squares, plus 2 strips, each 2.5 cm x 15 cm (1 in. x 6 in.)
- a pencil, scissors, white glue, waxed paper, a utility knife

1 Draw the outline of a tree on the white paper, as shown. Cut out the tree. This will be your pattern.

2 Lay your pattern on a piece of cardboard and trace around it. Repeat on the three other pieces of cardboard. Ask an adult to cut out the tree shapes using a utility knife.

3 On one tree, cut a notch from the top to halfway down its center. Make the notch twice as wide as the thickness of your cardboard. Repeat on another tree. On a third tree, cut a notch of the same width, from the bottom to halfway up the tree. Repeat on the remaining tree.

4 Glue the trees with the top notches together, lining up the notches. Glue the trees with the bottom notches together, lining up the notches.

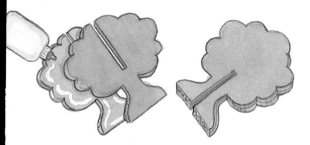

5 Draw a line where the treetop ends and the trunk begins. Ask an adult to cut through the thin top layer of the cardboard along this line on both sides of each tree. Peel this layer off the trunk.

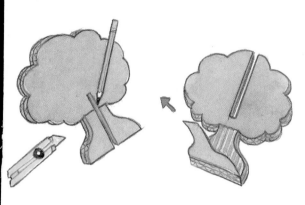

6 Glue a strip of tissue paper down the middle of each side of the unnotched treetop.

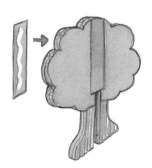

7 Glue your photos to both sides of the treetops. Do not paste them across the middle of the treetops.

8 Put a small amount of white glue on a piece of waxed paper. Poke the eraser end of your pencil into the center of one of the tissue paper squares, scrunch the tissue around the pencil and dip it into the glue. Stick the paper to your treetop. Do not cover the photos or the tissue paper strips. Continue until your treetop is covered. Place the paper "leaves" as close together as you can make them.

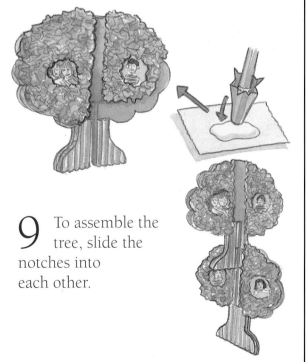

9 To assemble the tree, slide the notches into each other.

Booklet frame

A mini family album would make a great gift for Mom, Dad or a grandparent.

YOU WILL NEED

- 2 different-colored pieces of bristol board, one 15 cm x 66 cm (6 in. x 26 in.) and one 16 cm x 22.5 cm (6¼ in x 8¾ in.)
- 12 small photos
- felt markers
- 2 pieces of cord, each 15 cm (6 in.) long
- a ruler, a pencil, a utility knife, scissors, sticky tape, white glue

1 On the larger piece of bristol board, draw a line 10 cm (4 in.) from one of the short ends and score along it. Fold this small section back.

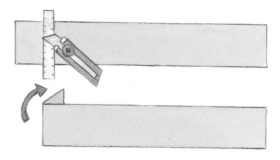

2 Turn the bristol board over. Lay the ruler along the edge of the small section and score a fold line. Fold this section back.

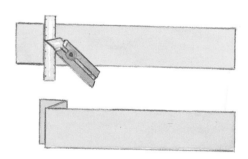

3 Repeat step 2 three more times. Trim the last section so that it is the same size as the others.

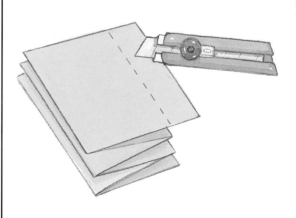

4 Fold open the frame and cut out opening shapes for two photos (see page 6) in each section. Leave a border at least 2 cm (¾ in.) wide around each opening. Tape your photos in place.

5 Lay the frame face down. If necessary, trim any photos that overlap the fold lines. Apply glue where shown and fold up the frame.

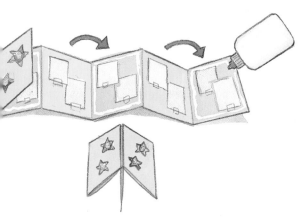

6 Decorate your frame using felt markers, crayons, stickers, etc.

7 To make a cover for the book, score a line 11 cm (4 ¼ in.) from each short end of the second piece of bristol board. Make two holes, each one 8 cm (3 in.) from the bottom of the bristol board and 1 cm (½ in.) from each side, as shown.

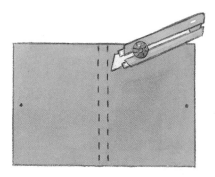

8 Fold the cover as shown. Thread a cord through each hole and tie a knot at the end. Place a dab of glue on each knot. Decorate the cover, insert the folded frame, and tie the cords.

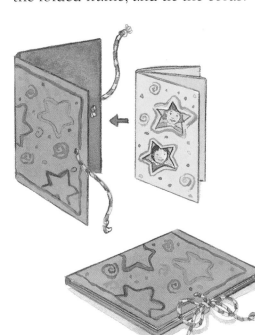

Woven ribbon frame

This frame is a great gift for your friends — make it with ribbons in their favorite colors.

YOU WILL NEED

- a photo, 10 cm x 15 cm (4 in. x 6 in.)
- 2 pieces of corrugated cardboard, each 25 cm x 30 cm (10 in. x 12 in.)
- 2 cm (¾ in.) wide ribbon: 11 pieces of one color, each 30 cm (12 in.) long, and 13 pieces of a different color, each 26 cm (10½ in.) long
- a pencil, a ruler, a utility knife, scissors, sticky tape, white glue

1 Draw a photo opening measuring 9.5 cm x 13.5 cm (3¾ in. x 5¼ in.) in the center of one piece of cardboard.

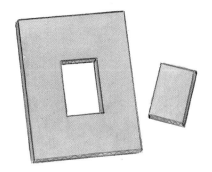

2 Measure and draw a line 6 cm (2¼ in.) from the opening on all four sides. Cut out the frame front along these lines. To make the frame back, place the frame front on the other piece of cardboard, trace around the outside edge and cut out the shape.

3 Set aside six ribbons of each color. Cut the rest of the ribbons in half.

4 To weave a cover for the frame, first attach the vertical ribbons. Place the end of a long ribbon at a corner of the frame as shown and fasten it with tape. Wrap the ribbon around the frame and tape to the back. Continue wrapping and taping the long ribbons, placing them so they touch but don't overlap. Use the shorter same-colored ribbons to wrap the frame opening. Cover the entire frame.

6 When you have finished weaving, place the frame face down on your work surface. Tape the ribbon ends to the back of the frame.

5 Weave in the horizontal ribbons. Slide a long, different-colored ribbon under the first vertical ribbon, over the second, under the third and so on. The second ribbon will go over the first vertical ribbon, under the second, etc. Use the shorter ribbons to weave around the frame opening.

7 Attach spacers and the frame back following the directions on page 9. Attach an easel back following the directions on page 7. Insert your photo.

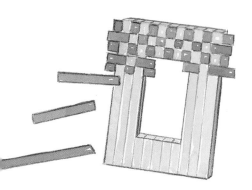

Column frame

You can make this frame look as if it's made of marble by mixing three or four colors while they are still wet.

YOU WILL NEED

- 2 cardboard tubes from paper towel rolls
- 16 plastic drinking straws
- 3 or 4 sheets of newspaper
- papier-mâché (see page 11)
- corrugated cardboard:
8 squares with sides 8 cm (3 in.) long and a rectangle 10 cm x 18 cm (4 in. x 7 in.)
- a photo 10 cm x 15 cm (4 in. x 6 in.)
- scissors, masking tape, white glue, 8 clothespins, paint, paintbrushes

1 To make the columns, cut the tube to the same length as the straws. Evenly space seven straws around each tube and tape them in place.

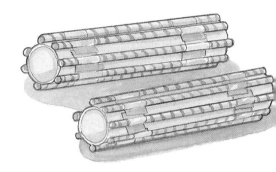

2. Tear one sheet of newspaper into small pieces. Dip it into the papier mâché and cover each column with two layers. Set the columns aside to dry.

3 Glue the squares of cardboard together in pairs so that you have four double-thick squares. Cover them with papier-mâché and let them dry.

4 To make rolls for the tops of the columns, cut out 16 strips of newspaper, each 5 cm x 23 cm (2 in. x 9 in.). Stack 4 strips on top of each other.

Fold them in half as shown.

Open them again.

Fold each long edge in to the center fold line.

Apply glue to one of the flaps on one side.

Fold the strip in half again.

5 Roll up both ends of the strip by folding them in on themselves four times and applying glue along the way. Hold each roll in place with a clothespin until dry. Repeat the stacking, folding, gluing and rolling with the remaining 12 strips to make 3 more column tops.

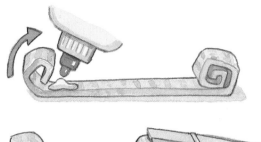

6 Center each column on a cardboard square so that one of the spaces between two straws faces one side of the square as shown. This will be your inside edge. Tape the column in place and apply papier-mâché to firmly attach the square to the column.

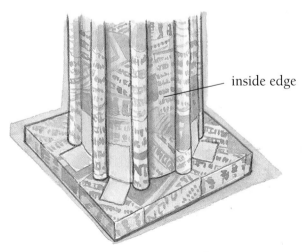

— inside edge

Instructions continue on the next page

7 Repeat step 6 to attach the tops to the columns. Set them aside to dry.

9 Glue the rolls to the top of each column. Let them dry, then paint the columns and the frame base.

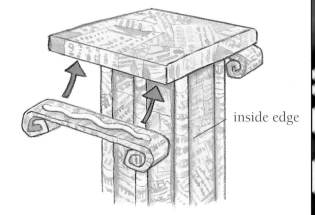

inside edge

8 To make the frame base, center a straw along each short edge of the cardboard rectangle and tape it in place. Cover the rectangle and straws with papier-mâché, but leave 2.5 cm (1 in.) at each end of the straws uncovered. Let dry.

10 Assemble the frame as shown. Mark the spot where the straws on the frame base touch the inside edge of each column. Carefully poke a hole in the column just large enough to fit the straw. Insert the straws and hold them in place with a dab of glue. Attach your photo to the frame base (see page 6).

Chalkboard frame

A fun way to display your class photo, this frame would also be a great gift for your favorite teacher.

YOU WILL NEED

- a class photo, 13 cm x 18 cm (5 in. x 7 in.)

- corrugated cardboard, 3 pieces 23 cm x 28 cm (9 in. x 11 in.), 4 pieces 8 cm x 28 cm (3 in. x 11 in.) and 2 pieces 2 cm x 34 cm (3/4 in. x 13 1/2 in.)

- 3 pieces of light cardboard, each 5 cm x 23 cm (2 in. x 9 in.)

- black poster paint

- a white pencil crayon

- 2 nails with large heads (roofing nails work well)

- masking tape, a ruler, a pencil, scissors or utility knife, white glue, a paintbrush

1 Tape your photo in the center of one of the large pieces of corrugated cardboard. You should have a 5 cm (2 in.) border on all sides of the photo. Follow steps 2 and 3 on page 8 to create your frame front.

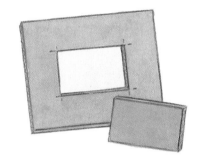

2 Glue the other two large pieces of corrugated cardboard together to make a frame back.

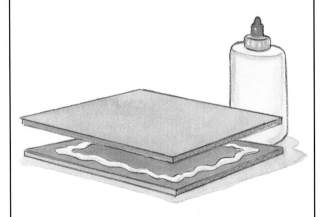

Instructions continue on the next page

3 Glue a piece of light cardboard along the outside edge of each short side of the frame back. These are spacers. Trim the third spacer to fit between them, and glue it in place along the outside edge.

4 Apply glue to the spacers and place the frame front on the frame back, lining up the edges. Place heavy books on the frame and let it dry.

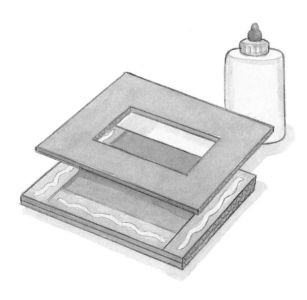

5 Paint the frame with black poster paint. When it is dry, use the white pencil crayon to decorate the frame front so it looks like a chalkboard. Make sure that the opening for your photo is at the top of your frame.

6 To make the stand for the chalkboard, glue two of the 8 cm x 28 cm (3 in. x 11 in.) strips of corrugated cardboard back to back. Repeat with the remaining two strips.

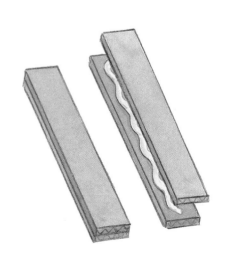

7 Draw two lines down the length of each strip. The lines should be 2.5 cm (1 in.) from each side of the strips. Mark a point 4 cm (1½ in.) from the bottom of each line. Connect the points with the closest corners of the strips. Cut out the shapes along the lines.

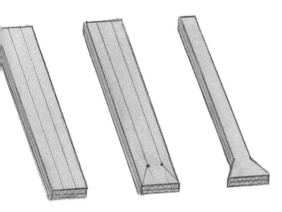

8 On each shape, measure 4 cm (1½ in.) in on its bottom and draw a line that is 2 cm (¾ in.) long. Make a cut on each side of the line, fold up the flap you just cut and trim it off. Use a nail to make a hole in the center of the shape 9 cm (3½ in.) from its top.

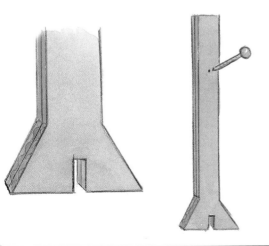

9 To make the base for the stand, glue the 2 cm x 34 cm (¾ in. x 13½ in.) strips together.

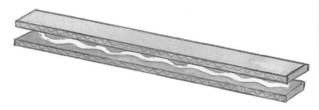

10 To assemble your chalkboard, line up the top of the frame with the top of the sides of the stand. Push the nails through the holes and into the middle piece of cardboard of your frame. Slide the base of the stand into the slots on the sides of the stand. Insert your photo.

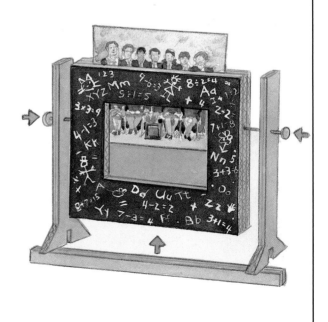

Quick and easy frames

Most of the frames shown on the next three pages can be made in just two steps. To display your finished frame, see page 7 for instructions on how to make an easel back or a hanging loop.

BRAIDED PIPE CLEANER FRAME

1 Braid three pipe cleaners together. Make a second braid using three more pipe cleaners, then lay the braids side by side and form them into a circle. Wrap them with more pipe cleaners as shown.

2 Cut out a construction paper circle just smaller than the pipe cleaner circle and attach your photo to it. Glue the pipe cleaner circle to the photo as shown. Add a pipe cleaner loop to hang your frame.

POPSICLE STICK FRAME

1 Stack and glue together 12 painted Popsicle sticks as shown.

2 Glue on beads or other decorations, and tape a small photo to the back of the frame.

HANGING FELT FRAME

1 Cut a photo opening in one end of a piece of felt and tape your photo in place. Apply glue to the edges of the felt and the back of the photo and fold the felt in half. Insert a pencil along the fold.

2 Decorate the frame and tie a ribbon to the pencil to hang your frame.

MARGARINE LID FRAME

1 Cover a margarine lid with strips of wrapping paper following the collage directions on page 11. Let it dry, then glue your photo to the lid.

2 Glue beads and buttons around the inside edge of the lid so that they cover the edges of the photo.

STYROFOAM FRAME

1 Cut a photo opening in a clean Styrofoam meat tray. Use a pencil to draw patterns on the Styrofoam, then paint your frame with acrylic paints.

2 Follow steps 4 to 7 on page 9 to make a frame back and insert your photo.

MAGNET FELT FRAME

1 Cut out two pieces of felt that are the same size. Cut a photo opening in one piece and tape your photo in place. Apply glue to the edges of the felt and the back of the photo and attach the second piece of felt.

2 Decorate the frame and glue a flat magnet to its back.

SEE-THROUGH FRAME

1 Cut out two same-sized pieces of acetate that are larger than your photo. Cut around the photo as shown. Place a small loop of sticky tape on the back of the photo and attach it to one piece of acetate. Place the second piece of acetate over the first, sandwiching the photo in between.

2 Wrap cloth tape around the sides of the frame.

WOODEN BLOCK FRAME

1 Trim your photo to fit a small block of 2 in. x 4 in. pine. Sand the edges of the wood and paint it with acrylic craft paint.

2 Place your photo on the wood and attach it with thumb tacks, just at the edges of the photo. Do not push the tacks through the photo — the tack head will hold the photo in place.

COLLAGE FRAME

1 Make a frame shape by gluing pictures cut from magazines or calendars onto a piece of bristol board. Brush on white glue thinned with water. Let it dry.

2 Cut out the frame and the photo opening. Tape your photo in place from behind. Make a frame back from another piece of bristol board and glue it to the frame front.

LACED-UP FRAME

1 Measure and cut a frame front and frame back, following steps 1 to 6 on pages 8–9. Wrap the frame front with gift wrap or brown paper, following the directions on page 10.

2 Use a hole punch to punch holes around the outside of the frame back. Using the frame back as a guide, punch holes in the same places on the frame front. Center your photo in the frame opening and fasten it with tape.

3 Use twine or ribbon to lace the frame front and frame back together, then decorate the frame.